Wild Hearts C

Wild Hearts Can’t Be Broken

Contents

Terrence Bey

These poems are dedicated to those who have been hurt, to those who understand they have hurt others and to those who want to never hurt again. Together we won't fold.

-never fold again

(Hope you enjoy these words I write for you and some of the illustrations I designed for you)

Wild Hearts Can't Be Broken

I'm grateful for you

Wild Hearts Can't Be Broken

My heart will no longer
be hung by a rope.
My love will never
be tamed by the
wrong.
Constant affection
won't be terminated
by default.
My desires will never
lead me blind.
I finally understand how
to breathe,
live and know
what I deserve. It's for me
to
be
WILD.

Terrence Bey

I keep my heart on safety,
because my love is like bullets.

Now,
recover from
those
scars.
So that you will
understand
how to be a better you
for the future.
Let old wounds
heal accordingly,
so you will
know which path
to go into,
in the
present.

I hope you remember that if the person is temporary, so is the pain they've cursed you with.

Wild Hearts Can't Be Broken

I sometimes don't like seeing your tattoos.
Marking old territory.
Ink that's filled
with memories and pastimes that have been
made
permanent.
Which you created and will be
a part of you forever,
with no room for me to fill.

-No Ink Crew

Terrence Bey

I was stuck and I didn't want to be selfish and
have you stick around.
I let go of your hand,
your body drifted away
like water flows down a stream or like it's being
grabbed by quicksand.

Wild Hearts Can't Be Broken

I trusted you with my body,
but I didn't trust you with my heart,
neither my soul.

Suffering over
someone that doesn't care about me
seems to be my happiness and
seems to be my life sometimes.

-killing me softly

I continue to fall in love
with people
who have extra baggage,
because I know I'm strong enough to
help them carry it.

-I am extra help

If I do all the things she has done before me,
Would she look at me the same?
Would she love me the same?
Would she understand me
as I've understood her?

-deep thinking

You deserve everything that life has to offer you.
Even when it seems like I can't offer you anything.
You already have everything.

-The sweetest thing 2002

When you're willing to drop everything for someone without hesitating.
No matter what the outcome means for you.
Because you want them to be happy.

-Love is

We don't just live in the now.
We fight through it,
which is why we are so strong.

-Bullying life

I'm simply crazy
about you.
I wake up thinking about you.
I will ignore every
phone call, because all I want to do is hear from you.
Even if I'm mad at you, I can't be for too long.
Sometimes I get bored and look at pictures of you on my wall.
There's something special about you,
but all I know is that God sent me something,
that's so damn beautiful.

-crazy but grateful

I wasn't there
to save you from all the bullshit
you never needed in your life.

-sorry babe

Terrence Bey

I always thought it would be easy to love.
I always thought it would be easy to
find the right one.
I always thought I would get married at an early
age and have kids right after.
I always thought that my first love
would be my last love.
But my thoughts have changed,
life has changed
and I focus on building
the new.

-*Overrated*

I finally see
that I should have
loved you a little
harder.

-can't replace time

Everyone you meet will be a part of your journey.
Not all of the people you meet are meant to stay in your life and that's ok.

-oh okay

Wild Hearts Can't Be Broken

The worst
feeling is letting your
guard down.
When you told yourself not to and now you have to wait to see how the ending will be.

-complicated mind

**Every brick they threw at me,
I used to build my castle
and I'm not even Prince Charming.**

-not an issue

I just wish that
we can put everything
behind us and just go.

-Panic

Burdens aren't usually that
bad when you have someone to share them
with.

If we all could love in the face of hate there would only be peace. When my people wake up, that's what they will see.

-feeling like Pac

Please don't take my attention for granted while I adore you.

-catch this vibe while I'm interested in you

Wild Hearts Can't Be Broken

My past always seems to catch up with me.
But by the time it does,
I've
already let time beautify
and heal me.
Now get lost!

Terrence Bey

I want to be your light
when you sleep at night.
I want to be the light in your
dreams that guide you when you're
having a nightmare.
I want to be the light that
wakes you up in the morning.
The light that hits through the windows
torturing your eyes to open.
Saving you from the succession of images that bother you.

-I can be what you need me to be

They say the truth comes out
when your drunk, but the truth
also shows when you're sober.

-Pay attention

I can't lose her.
With butterflies in my stomach.
I fear when the light in her eyes
has dimmed.

-consternation

Everyone seems to know your story, but nobody even knows theirs.

-cheers to the thinkers and opinionators

I try not to look back because every time I do
I have these conversations with myself
and I say…
"What the fuck was I thinking?!"

If we could all realize that death is upon us at any time
and understand tomorrow is not promised,
we would be able to understand
that we don't have time for the bullshit that consumes us.

-no diggity no doubt

We've all played the game and lost.

-don't lie

Wild Hearts Can't Be Broken

Your heart weakens,
your love hurts,
you say it stinks,
but we forget who wanted it first,
now drown beautifully.

I trusted you so blindly
and what really hurts
was when you showed me that I'm truly blind.

Vampire

You fell in love
with the dark
and you hide
away from the light.

A girl can always get what she wants, but it's not always exactly what she needs.

You will lose out on the person you should truly be with;
by choosing a person you think
could be the answer to all your
tempted needs.

*-Sex *Versus* Making Love*

You were hurt
because I broke away from you.
I was hurt once because they broke away from me.
And you will hurt them because you too will break away.

- Cycles

Never lose sight of those
who have your back and
continue to go hard for you.

-Strong Ties

I'll wait,
and when the time is right,
I know you will be there.

She's only protecting herself
with those thorns that have stabbed
you.

-She's Guarded

I came along and showed her different
and when my feet had been too wet,
I showed her exactly the same thing
that the fools before me had exposed her to.

Now I feel like a word being crossed out on
a drafted paper,
like when you make a mistake spelling a word,
with no eraser.

-another fool

The only person
that can hurt me
and I mean really hurt me,
is ME.

-Don't Underestimate Responsibility

Don't sweat it.
You have the best option.
Make your wants want you.

-Don't chase, don't beg, don't stress

Wild Hearts Can't Be Broken

I never needed you
to understand me,
but I was wondering if you
were willing to try.

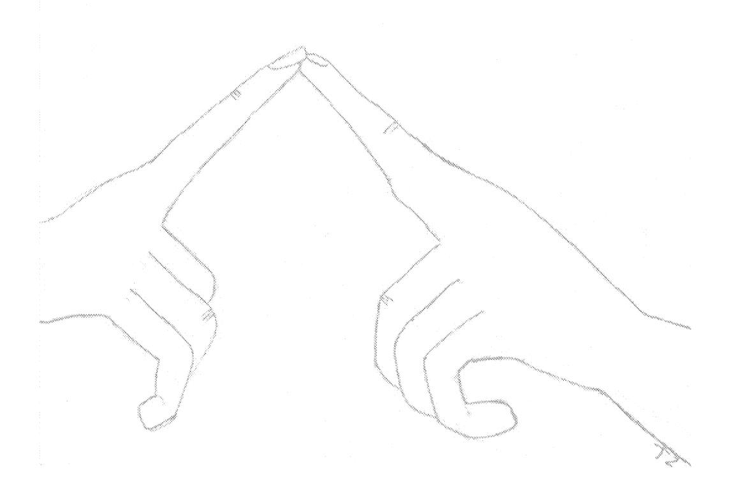

I never ask for love,
but I sure know how to
take it.

We as men seem to not value girls
that are beautiful and rare,
because we are blinded
by ugly spirits,
with sexual habits.

I entered her life
and
I was the one
who burned her past.
I picked up her heart
where the last man left it:
damaged and alone
on West 42[nd]street- Time Square.

-Commercial neighborhood beginning

I see you
practicing self-forgiveness,
holding yourself accountable, communicating
your needs
and accepting nothing less than what you
deserve.

-what growth looks like

Work and love,
you just have to keep them separate.
If you make it out,
with not keeping them separate,
all blessings to you two.

-never shit where you sleep

The worst feeling
is when you feel
love fading.
You can't understand why
and you continue to blame yourself,
for one's actions.

-losing interest

I will always care for you, but not as my person anymore.

There was this look
in her eyes.
Pure rage,
like there was something terrible
taken away from her
and in that moment I knew
it was me.
I stole a piece of her
happiness.

-jerk

The version of you I fell in love with does not exist anymore.

-so why should we exist?

They desire you,
but don't want
to value you.
It seems like their lost
and want things they
don't deserve.

I really just wanted to
apologize for putting you
through all that, which you didn't deserve.

-Dear Self

If every morning
you were able to
tell yourself
"I am
beautiful,
I've known weak,
but
I am strong",
you would be unstoppable.

-Positive Affirmation

**To be honest,
I haven't found
my equal.
To be honest my equal
hasn't found me, but
I do think about you
and how I am letting you
be free.**

-find your way to me

Pick your head up sis,
there is no need to beg for love
when someone out
there is praying
to be with someone like you.

-you're a prayer

There is power
in rediscovering
your own voice.

Every second of the day
I wish I can remind you of your
own worth.

-You show me the
beauty in what we are…

I will never betray your trust,
I would never hurt you,
I want you to know of this.

-to my Ace

Honestly, I like being alone
so if I want you around,
I must love your energy.

-keeping it 100

I want love that's eternal,
the one
you play
for keeps.

**Everyone is fighting their
own battle,
just as you are fighting yours.**

-walking through Harlem

**Bring me to my climax,
without sex.**

-give it to me after

I really don't play about her,
because I was really made for her!

-On God!

Speak loud when you are
angry with her,
and you'll be having your last
SPEECH.

-speak wisely

You emptied the clip

**You broke my heart,
you got me on savage mode.
I made a promise to myself,
that I will never fold.**

-Feeling like "Tommy from POWER"

I woke up this morning
and realized that life has to go on,
with you or without you.

-life too short

My love life
is crippled,
but still I stand
and still I walk.

One of the weirdest things in the world is to still love someone after they stop loving you.

-the risk of loving too hard can be sad

I need you to choose
me with a full heart
now.

-no second chances

I've buried things that
I'm not proud of
and it affected me in ways I can't explain.

-set it off

I hope you're not having great meaningless sex with your new friend.

-selfish being

When I date you my goal is to marry you,
build with you, understand you, grow with you,
nothing less, only to give you more.

-I've searched 40,075 km for your love
and I still couldn't find it,
maybe I'm searching
on the wrong planet.

The opportunity had opened
in gentle winds,
so I left my guarded walls
and climbed up hers with high risk
every time I saw her.

-persistent

That text you get,
the one that has you cheesing like you never did before, because all your used to are
frowns and cold storms.

-Electrifying

They leave a dent on your heart
and a bad taste in your mouth.
They undervalue friendships...
They are called "Cantankerous."

-fall back with that negative energy

**I don't know what I would do
without your type
of love.**

-idk

As men
we seem to not realize that
real women are hard to come by and we might
not ever realize it until it's
too late.

You don't have to be the jack of all trades sweetie, someone is waiting to help you out, but for now help yourself.

-Hold it down

We both risked it all and we both lost.

-shit isn't always good as it seems

Terrence Bey

Those who guard their hearts
so tight are not waiting for a
better thief, but waiting for a thief that wants to
change themselves
for them.

-Blue Streak '99

In deep thought
standing on the train platform
at Astor place.
I try to remember 1 year ago,
when everything was still fresh,
where I was able to pass all tests and love was only building up like Jenga.

-missing that brand new love

I left even though
I was still in love with you.
Only to protect you
from the future hurt.

-You deserve better than me

Be selfish with me, but just me.

-It's mutual,
*let's enjoy the f*ck out*
of each other

I want my love to feel the same way
I feel when I can't wait to wear new
clothes I bought...

-let that sink in

I am thankful
for the bad that enters my life,
it always helps open my eyes
to see the good things
that I wasn't paying attention to before.

Don't shrink yourself,
to fit into places
you've outgrown.

-we don’t do that

Why stay in the fire with someone
when you can escape and get out?
You're losing oxygen and
the density of the heat is high.
You have time to run,
but you will still fight to save that dreadful
love.

I'm terrified that I may never get over you, even if you are certainly over me.

When two waves don't ride anymore,
when those signals don't
intersect,
you were just somebody I use to know.

-Guard your heart

Father figure

He stumbled upon
a few hearts laying down.
He stitched their broken spirits back together.
He picked up all the bags that he had seen on the floor and he put them on his back.
He was the rebuilder for what that family was missing.

-Rare Men

I've learned that nothing
in this world is really ours,
so it's perfectly fine to let it go.

-everything belongs to mother nature

A good soul
will always find a good home.

Wild Hearts Can't Be Broken

You want me, but you're playing a dangerous game.
Are you finished hoeing around?
Are you ready to make a change?
Are you ready to put your grownup pants on and hustle with me?
Cause I'm about chasing that bag.

-Money Team

She's been solid before she became his home.

-everyman needs

Wild Hearts Can't Be Broken

She came back home,
scrubbed the
dirt off her skin
and the dirt underneath her nail beds.
She was in the shower
for a long period of time and
wanted to cuddle. She wrapped her arms around
me and made me feel like I was needed, and
I was her completion.

**When you talk about raising
kids, and having a house,
it's the most appealing thing.**

-Plans

She saw his struggle, so she anchored his survival.

-Strong Willed

**Hoping my lover
will not help me self-destruct,
but help me reconstruct and elevate.**

-give me uplifting vibes

Don't hide from the feeling.
That will be your first step to healing.

Pain traps the mind like quicksand,
patience and breathing will grab your hand.

You are loved,
so don't focus
on the people
who don't love you.

-YKTV

**I'm out working late, running through traffic,
I’m feenin’ to get to your body because I want to
speak its language.**

-warmth cravings

Don't wait too long on the sideline for the coach to see your potential. Make sure you can get in the game and have some appreciated minutes and consistency.

-Side Chick Hope

There is nothing wrong with you, if you think you have failed today, get up and try again.

Fall in love with the process of building yourself back up.

Some pieces that fell shouldn't be picked back up.

-Leave that Shit right there

I hope you believe that you are so much more than what has been done to you.

Just a reminder to let go and submerge yourself in the rawness of your emotions.

-release, feel, & heal

When they choose someone else over you, you need to choose yourself the next time they try to come back around.

-No free meals sneaky

Open the door of self-worth affirmations and they will lead you to doors you've always had around you. Believe in yourself, accept yourself for who you are. Opportunities are always open, growth is continuous. Be grateful for the amazing things in your life, and congratulations on being ready to open the new doors.

When they keep throwing you in the toy box
and stuffing you in the closet. They pick and
choose when it's convenient to take you out.
Position yourself like a soldier,
put your armor on,
and let them know you are moving on.

-break a toxic cycle

I hear you when you say you love me but I need proof that you got me.

-actions

There's a place for us
out there and no one can tell us, who to be, what to do, when to leave, where to go, why we leave and tell us how to get there.

-WHO, WHAT, WHEN, WHERE, WHY and HOW

Smelling the sheets
that smell like you,
as I wake.
Where you left
an empty space.

Everything I love is kept quiet.
Privacy is safety,
and fake love made my heart
empty.

Your taste in love changes when you start loving yourself.

-Issa vibe

Babe I know you're exhausted.
But breathe,
this is not your full story,
this is only one chapter.

Before you give anyone a second chance, give yourself a chance first.

Wild Hearts Can't Be Broken

**We argued,
and overtime
those arguments
became lessons.
Time conquers all
then we fell into depression.
Buttons always pressing,
there was pride and never really confessions.
There's someone else in the game because I
threw an easy interception.**

-Bad NFL Reception

**She was his rose,
yet her petals
fell off.**

Why are you looking
for answers in others, and not answers from me.
Why aren't you looking for answers that are in
yourself, instead of chasing these streets?

I stopped expecting things from people, and ever since that day I've stopped being disappointed.

Wild Hearts Can't Be Broken

I've been working my way up this mountain so I can reach you.
But,
I am scared of heights and
I am scared of falling.

Instead of ignoring somebody when you're mad, how about you be mature and start communicating.

-if you real right

They will talk about you,
because they don't have an answer for putting you down.

-they fear you

You have taken all the steps, you have made all those prayers,
yet you want to stay,
when they are really whispering in your ears
“leave me alone & let me go.”

-Almost Doesn’t Count Brandy

Wild Hearts Can't Be Broken

To the old me.
I miss you dearly,
I was struck by pain and shit hurt me severely.

-Hood Scars on me

It's not just the money I'm after.
It's the freedom to live life on my own terms
with you.

-the goal for us

**There's no need
to address shade
from trees with
no fruit.**

-noted

I think it's true
that we all have that one person
we would take back,
no matter the pain
they installed in our heart.

-Let me really think about that, nah I'm good

It's beginning to feel normal again,
I take deep breaths
and understand the beauty of wind.

Alone.
She's willing to start over,
through lessons of hurt, to build
her castle that she dreamed of when she
watched those Disney Princess Movies.

Wild Hearts Can't Be Broken

People try to grow a connection with me and I throw it away.
It's not intentional.
I try to grow a connection with people and they end up throwing me away.
So I guess it's not intentional.

I used to return energy,
and now I just remove myself.

-distance response completed

We can't help hurting the wrong people.

-Sadly insane

How can you wake up
and smile through all that pain?
You've been drenched in storms with all that rain,
but I see in the end it will become your gain.
Cause you've already changed to a brand new page.

-life goes on sis

There's nothing like a woman that can nurture you with lessons and empower your growth.

-Real Men Say Amen

Our hearts are flammable when
we can't receive a text back from our significant
other. “Like, do I play with you like that?”

-

Who more important than me?

Her eyes promised me tomorrow.

**Don't betray yourself
by forgetting about yourself.**

I got a 90's R&B type of heart.
Can you match that?

Finding both love and friendship in one person is rare.

-You'll know

Someone told me
you were worrying less about everyone else,
and focusing more on yourself.
I think that's always beautiful.

Never disappoint a woman
multiple times and expect her to match your
frequency.

One day you will
love yourself
a little deeper
and understand that
this world was not given to you
by man but by chance.
A chance,
for you to be whatever you want or desire.

Sometimes
I fall in love
with people before they are entirely
ready to be loved.

-Shit Happens

The best ways to heal
is by getting everything out.
So communicate.
Even if it's uneasy.

-Try a little tenderness
60's Flow

Terrence Bey

I would never think
that I was someone who leaves.
Never thought there was an end
to my patience, forgiveness or the chances I gave.
But I guess everyone has their limitations.

I've admired the fire,
and I also have been
brave enough to
put my bare hands
in the flames.

**We have to stop trying to
fix these people
who don't mind breaking us.**

-Stop choosing what isn't choosing you

All I want to hear is
"you're the best thing that has ever happened to me" and have them mean it.

-Listening to Drake "Best I Ever Had"

Terrence Bey

My soulmate is out
there living her best life,
while I'm probably dealing with someone
who really doesn't appreciate me.
Hurry up
and rescue me mate.

-Australian Accent

Wild Hearts Can't Be Broken

Even when you feel ugly,
you're sexy,
cute,
beautiful,
gorgeous and
exquisite
to someone who sees you for you.

Bro,
speak life into your woman, she probably goes through battles that you can't even fathom.

-Encourage her,
that soul different

Can we level up and learn from each other?

-Simple Happy Life

If you see me less,
that means I'm doing more,
and just remember you chose to walk out the door.

The falling part is easy,
it's the Un-falling part that is hard.

-(SWV Weak Vibes vs Not gone Cry Mary J Vibes)

Terrence Bey

If you can stop talking to me,
and just let me heal.

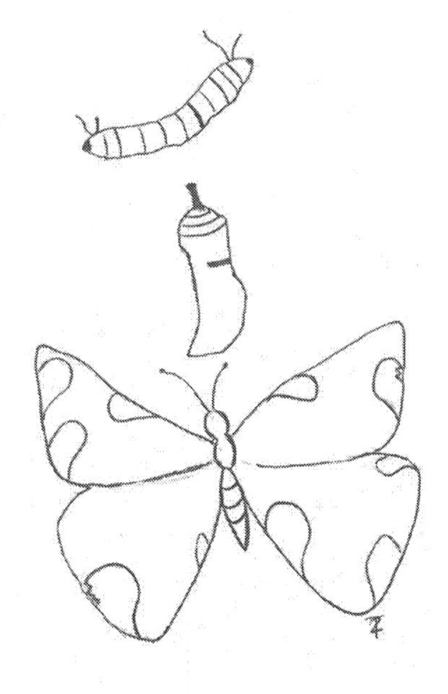

I react on feelings without really
thinking.
Sorry for the pressure in advance.

-Some-Times

Terrence Bey

I'm alone. I didn't choose this,
it actually chose me.
For the better,
I have grown.

**I know who's going to give you everything you want in life,
your damn self!**

-work hard towards what you want, all you need is you

I see you trying to carry the weight of the world on your shoulders.
I know that a lot of this is your fault and some of it is not.
When you finally realize the choices and decisions you have made could have been different, you will understand your power in the world, and change it.
You are your own boss.

-The art of choice (You are the creator)

Heal and continue.

-You got this

He collected hearts like trophies.
With every trophy
lies a story with crushed
souls.
His retaliation, him regaining control, him
coping with the hollowness
that his first love left in him.
It would soon come to crush him again by
another.

Her vicious cycle
of crushing hearts,
Is so she can regain hers.

-collecting souvenirs

She understands her worth
but will give you all of her.
She will give enough chances, until that last
chance is ready to be expired
and she will just let go.

-Hint: Appreciate Her

Wild Hearts Can't Be Broken

I can't stand to see you
with another man.

I can't stand to see you
utilizing our plans.

I see you smiling a lot more and I know you're
probably happy where you are.

But don't act like I never loved you
or act like I never had your back.
I would shut down my life for you again
and would try to keep it all intact.

-Confessions Part 3,
(rocking to Usher Confessions Album)

Is it crazy that a man will cheat on you and still look out for you?

-Crazy Alright!

I refuse to speak on how deeply in love I am with you sometimes, but know my heart beats your name.

-Tell Them You're Occupied

The worst feeling is when you're not talking to each other and you both really want to explode, because you have so much to tell each other, but you don't.

-Hi Pride,
I miss my Best Friend

My last relationship hurt me more
than I thought it did,
and I'm sorry for being so selfish,
as you were just trying to be my friend.

When they leave
like it's just nothing.
Especially when you didn't ask for any of it.
Makes you want to smack the dawg shit out of them.

-Get Smoked

Wild Hearts Can't Be Broken

After being alone for so long.
We find a heart.
We find a home.
We get attached, and
then it burns.
Then we tell
ourselves we won't ever do it again.

-Press Repeat

Terrence Bey

She's drained and she's tired.
I tend to see the good in her.
But she can't see the good in herself.
She's been heartbroken and mistreated,
but
I know that I'm good for her health.

I'm sorry we couldn't make it.
I hope you find your faith in me one day,
I will miss you always.

-bumping "There it is" by: Ginuwine

God sometimes gives me things that I cannot ignore,
like the first time I saw you.

My struggle became our struggle
and she wasn't afraid to stick around.

-Wife Material

Every time I look in her eyes
I feel as if we
are about to have a heavy
conversation in French.

**I've finally felt like I have mastered the art of being thoughtful, patient, and conscious.
It starts with me thinking about other's feelings before I react.**

-mindful and aware

Those who choose to stay despite all of our flaws are the ones who truly love us.

-no matter what

Wild Hearts Can't Be Broken

You can let your person know when their words
have hurt you,
admit their actions have hurt you,
admit you care about them,
and admit you have cried when you felt
unwanted.
You define bravery.

If she's the human who gives you butterflies in your stomach, love her to the core.

-Shitting Me

We could always stop playing games, travel the world, eat good food, lay on beautiful beaches, and break night.

-Come speak my language

Have you felt broken?
Just wanted someone
who stays when the morning came and look at
you like
you weren't just another mistake.

I like to be fly and I want my shawty to be fly.
We fly together.

-high fashion relationship

**It does the heart good,
when someone comes
along and tells you that you guys are a match
made in heaven, that you look good together
and that you deserve each other.**

-but that feeling…

Wild Hearts Can't Be Broken

I used to think she was
just another fish in the sea,
until she helped me realize
that she was always meant to be my sea.

All we want is a fresh breath of air, which makes us happy.

-come in fresh

We weren't meant to be
just like your
past.

-let's try things differently

When women love they really love with all their heart. If you show them attention, they will show you all the attention in the world. What you give them, they will give you more, but once women are disrespected or mistreated and it continues to happen, they will check out. When she checks out there's no getting her back. There's no coming back. You might as well look at her back, because that's the last thing you'll probably ever see.

-you needed to hear this

Yesterday's argument won't stop today's communication. Let's keep loving each other.

-What's the Vibe ?

If they hang up on you, they have said enough.

-Copy, Cool.

My mind made me walk away, while my heart silently said
turn around and fight for her.

I hate when our eyes meet and I instantly remember those feelings and see everything I lost with you.

You are not crazy
for wanting what you deserve,
scream it so they can hear it in the back!

I see you,
as someone that
is too important to lose.

-need someone like this

When she walks in the room, heads turn and necks crack,
because she is that
beautiful source of light
that wakes you.

-HER

I can see you,
you exist,
but you're only in my rearview.

You are proof that anyone can get through something devastating.

Your anxiety won't fool you into thinking that you can't achieve your dreams. You won't let anxiety fool you into thinking you're not strong enough for something.
You won't let anxiety convince you that you are not liked or loved. You won't let anxiety tell you something is wrong with you. This is not how you will be for the rest of your life, because if you're reading this you just took back control of your life, and won't let anxiety take control of you again.

-Bye Anxiety. I'm aware.

**I'm focused on the glow up,
staying busy,
making money,
growing the hair right,
skin life,
and
being happy these days,
hate me or love me.**

-Hate me now Nas Flow

I can't show you where it hurts but I feel something in my chest, where the Henny rest.

-How much you got on the henny?
The Henn-Dawg

That beginning consistency isn't cutting it, I need it throughout the whole book.

-You deserve consistency and not for one chapter

**If your absence brings me peace,
obviously you know I didn't lose you.**

Someone can only give you what you're willing to accept.

-Word to everything

The world deserves you
and I see all those colors hidden within you, but
yet you
are not ready to shine.
No rainbow, sun, nor diamond has any
competition with you.

All she wants is a man
that's fully committed to her.

-Period.

The ones that make you feel gorgeous and let you know they are there for you. The ones who are too busy to talk about other people because they are excited talking about visions, ideas, and goals for the year are my kind of people.

-best types of beings

I want to be your happy place.

**I pray that you become filled with so much happiness
that it heals every part of you.**

**All those scars are not meant
for everyone to see, those that truly love you
can see them and how beautiful they've made
you.**

Terrence Bey

Be in love with your stretch marks.
Be in love with your shape.
Embrace those sexy hips,
keep those curves right in place.
Your presence is something eyes won't ever
seem to miss, because you are beauty and
beauty still exists.

Wild Hearts Can't Be Broken

She sits on the floor bewailing about her not being pretty enough, about her being fat and not skinny enough. Being rejected by model agencies because her skin is not clear enough, too much plump, she's so fucking thick, mascara falling from her eyes because society doesn't give a fuck.
Tearing down her confidence. You thought that was a real prize?
She's worth every photo.
You can't paint brush God's real size.
Be in love with your stretch marks, be in love with your shape, your beauty still exists and it's right in front of your face.

-Full story (keep the faith)

I know one day there will be someone to come pick up all the broken pieces and cherish all the broken parts, and go by the name "Love."

Shower her with POSITIVITY.

I'm in love with listening to your heartbeat.

-I'm on you frozen like a mannequin

She makes me want to give her the world
without thinking
twice.

-infinity

They watched me die when
they could have saved me.
I watched them die and it felt
amazing.

-Karma

Wild Hearts Can't Be Broken

I was sick of the lies,
I was sick of the fakeness,
I was sick of being tired.
Cause all I feel is hate.
I played by the rules and I played on the faith.
I seemed to have come in second, and that was never my place.

I realized love was not for us.

-get rid of what no longer serves you

I'm off the edge of my bed just like I'm off the edge of my heart.

The problem wasn't that you didn't know me anymore,
the problem was that I didn't want to know you anymore.

-End of the Road
(Boys ll Men vibes)

Dear Judgmental People,

You never know what someone is going through, whether it's
personal or heartbreak.

-Can you even fit their shoe size?

I understand your jealousy,
because once you thought
you were better than me.

-times change

Everyday should be Valentine's Day when two souls make the choice to be inseparable.

-Jamming to "Love" by: Musiq Soulchild

Terrence Bey

I couldn't sleep right
because dreams were tight.
Waking up from the dead
and ready to fight.
I wear my heart on the sleeve,
and I think it's right.
You taught me some things
when my heart was on ice.
Hoping that I find you now,
before it's my time.

-She Something Special

Not everyone can dish out the same amount of love like you.

-Your My Favorite Soul

I'm willing to give you 100 percent with zero expectation of receiving anything in return.

Your love for another human inspires broken hearts.

Terrence Bey

Just because you can't see me
doesn't mean I'm not there.
I will always be beside you, in
your thoughts, in your dreams, and through the
drift, it's like air.

-Novembers rest
(Bethany K & Harold M)

When you're mad
I hope I can still
at least make your
heart
& body smile.

It's time for you to take a stand, it might be the toughest thing you have to do and it starts with you.

-big ups

**"Good morning Ugly"
means you are actually beautiful &
"Good morning punk" just means you are my punk,
and I adore you.**

-don't trip homie

I want to take care of you.
I want to take care of your soul,
you heart and your well-being.
Now let us grow old.

I love you like the last vision or dream I'll ever see.

-till death

If we all can heal the broken child in us,
we would be able to let the healthy adults grow out of us.

Quitting is not an option when it comes to you.

-Mindset

Real love is not there for you at your best,
it's there for you at your worst.

Wild Hearts Can't Be Broken

She's been a savage
but her heart is full of gold.
If you're seeking treasures
dare to be bold.
There's no time to waste,
love her,
as you help make her whole.
She too good for someone
that isn't really sure.

-Yo (Excuse Me Miss)

**It's always going to be easy to be wanted,
but I know I'd rather be valued.**

Never go back to a person who will never be waiting for you to return.

No one is going to hurt you ever again.

-believe in you

You are allowed to feel broken, and
you become dangerous when you learn how to
control those feelings.

My heart used to be owned by me until it became full of you.

-don't empty please

Don't become a version of the person that hurt you.

-You know that

I will chase her even after she's already mine.

This love I have for you
is worth more than this argument.

-let her know bro

The hardest thing is realizing you're not the best person for the one you thought you loved most in this universe, and knowing it's about to be your time to go.

-feelings fade

I stopped letting people paint me
with the colors
of their
choice.

Cheating on you would just be me cheating myself.

I never wanted to be that guy to leave you on
your own. I hope that you are doing well and I
hope that your heart is pure and warm.
Our souls are disconnected, but I can still hear
your moans. My escape I pictured beautiful but
now I'm all alone.
I always said that cheating you would've been
me cheating myself. Now I write my wrongs,
cause today I see you happy with someone else.

The most important things
to do is respect her,
love her,
give her everything and take her everywhere
except for granted.

-LET THE CHURCH SAY AMEN

You're
hoping I fall down and I'm praying you get on your feet.
We're not the same.

-growth on top of growth

You once drowned in negativity,
and pulled yourself up to the deck full of positivity.
I think that's dope.

-you controlled hope

When you look in the mirror you see your
competition.
When you truly understand that,
you'll begin to understand your purpose and
vision.

It hits differently when your efforts are ignored.

-Shit Sucks

She's just a little bit too perfect
and she has always been worth it!

Sit back and watch me be your peace, stop tripping, I don't want to leave, unless you want me to leave.

-Your peace, not piece of shit

Say my name, say my name,
when everyone is around you, let my name be your truth.

-Destiny Child Vibes

**I'm matching your words with your actions, put that time in
and keep rapping.**

-back it up

If you're reading this, never put yourself in a position that can lead you to question your self-worth as a person.

-self-esteem check

**His slogan was
"cuff her the right way and keep her the right way."**

-Grown man status

**She chose to be single.
She didn't have an attitude,
she just realized her worth
and let it be known
that she has high standards
and was okay to be alone.
She wasn't in a rush
to find him
so she kept doing her thang.**

-Patience is worth it

I need to find you
to
heal you
with you
to
be you
with you
just you,
alone.

-our journey alone

Block their number,
and enjoy your
summer,
fall,
winter,
spring,
and forever.

I made a promise to myself that I wouldn't let my loneliness reconnect me with toxic people.

-don't drink poison because you're thirsty

You weren't too busy denying your mistakes.
You started to learn, plant and grow.

You are being picky now
and still managing to
pick the wrong ones.
It's time you take special care of yourself.

I'll love someone
who will always
have a fear of losing me
or
I'll love someone
who never gives
me a fear of losing them.

-let's fear together or let's not fear at all

Go vibe with someone
who actually likes you.

-

Stop worrying about the attention
you don't receive

Wild Hearts Can't Be Broken

We fall,
we break.
We don't fail,
because then
we rise,
we heal,
we find strength,
we overcome,
we learn,
and we tell someone the story
to save the next.

-The Marathon Continues

Things can be easy with us, but you make things so hard. Stand strong or lay down and let me catch your vibe.

-Be professional or Be Nasty

My words might not mean anything to you right now,
but babe I want you
to know that you're worth it all.
I want you to know it's not meant for everyone's eyes to see
and it's not meant for every soul to understand.

-you worth fighting for

The beautiful thing about who you are,
is that you are the kind of person who decides
to love hard, even with a fragile heart.

-Good Person

I never meant to
hurt your feelings bro,
but not every girl is
replaceable.

- if you really understand how feelings flow.

I would say it's better to be single, than to be taken for granted.
But maybe being taken for granted
is a lesson for the both of you.
For you the one that's hurting,
and for you the one
who is still learning
how to actually care.

-

Perspective (Third Party)

Commitment and consistency.

-Valuable

When my assets are paying for my lifestyle,
I will call that real success.
It comes at a price
with me trying to be
my best.

-I just want to create some nests

Move how you are going to move.
Just know I'll move
accordingly.

-I'm on big energy and big frequency type of time

The version of a person who looked so happy with a certain somebody, may not be the same version of a person you get.

-Be careful what you ask for

Beautiful souls, always stay solid,
never let them see you fold,
keep yourself right
and the right
company close.

I hope you find love and happiness in yourself first.
Then you will truly be at peace.

Once you are at your lowest from that brokenness, you will stand up again.
You will have finally collected all those shattered pieces worth picking up and put yourself back together.
You will have finally found courage and confidence.
You will be healed.
"I want you to remember one thing and that is that
Wild Hearts Can't Be Broken."

Special Thanks To:

Editor: Katie Byrne
Editor: Nicole Pellerona
Editor: Jeanette Barnwell
Editor: Rrezarta Xhaferi
Graphic Designer: Albert Tubac
Graphic Designer: Tauheed
Art: Davide Zamberlan

To all that inspired me and never gave up on me, this book couldn't be done without you.
-Family, Friends, and Readers/Supporters

**Thank you for reading
with your mind,
heart, and soul.**

You beautiful being,
stay humble.
Stay positive,
keep learning,
keep growing,
be you,
be grateful.

-Creator of your life

Wild Hearts Can't Be Broken

Wild hearts can't break

Illustrations by: Terrence Bey

ISBN: 9781687341365

Terrence Bey
101 North Brand Boulevard, 11th Floor,
Glendale, California 91203,

www.Terrencebey.com

Made in the USA
Middletown, DE
23 November 2020